SPIRITUALS
FOR CHURCH AND CONCERT

Arranged by Phillip McIntyre

Table of Contents

These selections may be sung one octave lower for altos, or two octaves lower for basses.

H. T. FitzSimons Company
One of the Fred Bock Music Companies

Foreword

A music as powerful and as loved as the Negro spiritual could not be limited to its rudimental beginnings — a folksong. The spiritual through the years has developed in many directions. Among those developments are the arranged spiritual for choir and the arranged spiritual for solo voice and piano. In the late 1800's the Negro spiritual's development was stimulated by the Fisk Jubilee Singers' performance of these songs as they toured the United States. These songs, which seemed doomed to decline, were led back to popularity. Other choirs began to sing them and as a result composers of the period began arranging these songs for choir.

Harry Thacker Burleigh, however, was the first to arrange and perform spirituals in the style of the European art song. Burleigh regarded his efforts at composition as merely mental exercises. He was virtually forced by friends to publish "Deep River" in 1917. This resulted in Burleigh's fame as a composer. His influence in this form was wide-spread. Composers for generations would model their arrangements after this new style for which he was responsible. Great singers followed his tradition by including spirituals in the recital repertoire. Notable among these would be Marian Anderson, Roland Hayes, and Paul Robeson, each who coached with Harry Burleigh.

A new composer has emerged as a curator of this American art form. Phillip McIntyre's arrangements express the essence of this music in the tradition of the great spiritual arrangers. In this volume of songs you will be given another opportunity to immerse yourself into the culture of a people and a great American tradition.

William Warfield
Champaign, Illinois
January, 1990

Preface

The music of the Negro slave in the United States, the Negro spiritual, resulted in a human expression that is of a universal nature. These songs speak of hope, pain, suffering, joy, and other life experiences paralleled in the lives of all people. These songs do not express hatred. They do not seek revenge. They do not convey a negative attitude toward mankind. It was through these songs that the slaves expressed their inner emotions and relationship to God. The spiritual is a simplistic musical application to a complex theological or scriptural ramification or declaration. We are aware of the "double meanings" of many of the spirituals. Yet, these interpretations are secondary to their religious and theological meanings. These songs must be interpreted with an understanding of the origins, empathy with their originators, and a sense of a greater Being.

The musical interpretations of the songs in this volume must be approached from a sacred standpoint. The performers must bring to these songs sincerity. These songs must be studied, pondered over, sung, and resung until the meaning and true interpretation become evident to the singer *and* accompanist. These songs must not be taken lightly. They should not imitate poor examples of performances of spirituals. An authenticity of the music should be sought. This does not include overly articulated dialect or exaggerated rhythms. Improvisation in these songs is not necessary. All the tools that one will need to make the songs in this volume effective to the listener are on the printed page. The performers' goal must be to meet the challenge to recreate with integrity the music on the score, thus recreating a great art form.

Phillip McIntyre
Washington, D.C.
January, 1990

About the Arranger

PHILLIP McINTYRE has distinguished himself not only as a composer and arranger, but also as an educator, conductor, church musician, and concert organist. He is a graduate of The Catholic University of America in Washington, D.C., where he received undergraduate and graduate degrees in music. McIntyre has held several posts in church music and has taught on the high school and university levels. He presently pursues a career as a church musician and college instructor. In addition, he is sought after as a conductor, clinician, and concert organist. He has performed at the John F. Kennedy Center for the Performing Arts in Washington, D.C.; Morehouse College in Atlanta, GA; Knoxville College in Knoxville, TN; Christ Church Cathedral in St. Louis, MO; the National Shrine of the Immaculate Conception and the Washington Cathedral, also in Washington, D.C.

to Leontyne Price

I WANT TO BE READY

TRADITIONAL SPIRITUAL
Arranged by Phillip McIntyre

Lively, but not too fast
M.M. ♩ = ca. 69

O, I want to be read - y. O, I want to be read - y.

I want to be read - y, Lord, to walk in Je - ru - sa - lem just like John. O,

just like John.
1. Well John said the cit - y was just four square;
2. I've nev - er been to heav-en, but I've been told;

* higher note for repeats

F0114

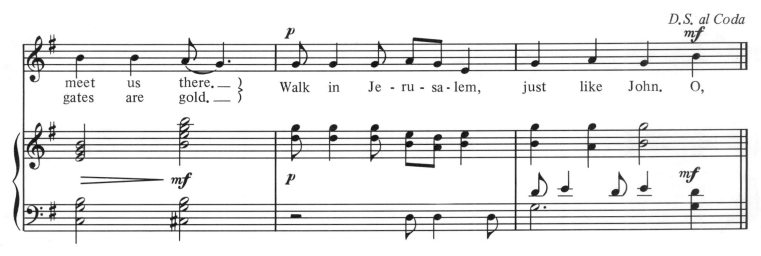

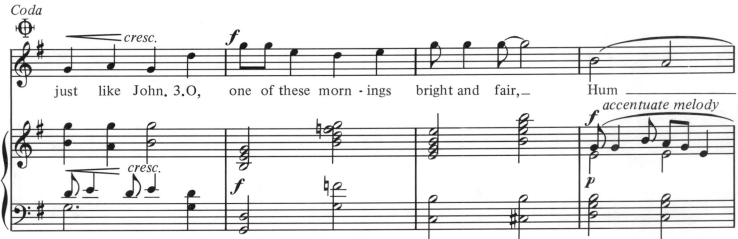

5

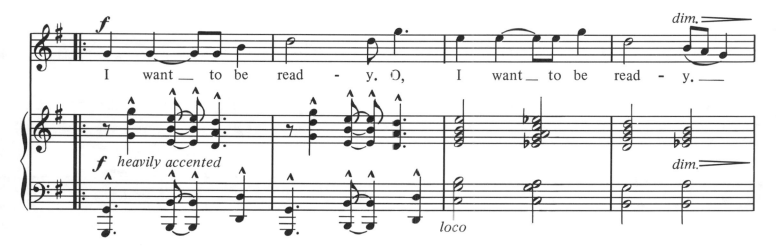

I want to be read-y. O, I want to be read-y.

I want to be read-y to walk in Je-ru-sa-lem just like John. O,

talk in Je-ru-sa-lem, sing in Je-ru-sa-lem, shout in Je-ru-sa-lem,

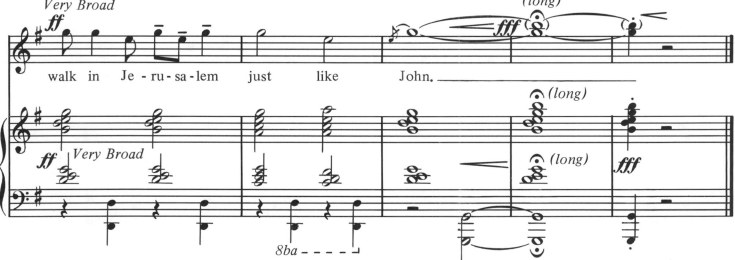

walk in Je-ru-sa-lem just like John.

in memory of my mother, Louise McIntyre

SIT DOWN SERVANT, SIT DOWN!

TRADITIONAL SPIRITUAL
Arranged by Phillip McIntyre

* Final chorus use higher notes.
** After final chorus go to Coda
*** know= I know

F0114

* higher notes for 2nd verse

to William Warfield

LORD, I WANT TO BE A CHRISTIAN

TRADITIONAL SPIRITUAL
Arranged by Phillip McIntyre

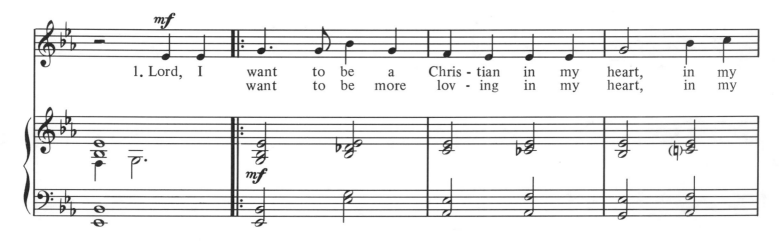

1. Lord, I want to be a Chris-tian in my heart, in my
   want to be more lov-ing in my heart, in my

heart.— Lord, I want to be — a — Chris-tian in my heart.———
heart.— Lord, I want to be — more — lov - ing in my heart.———

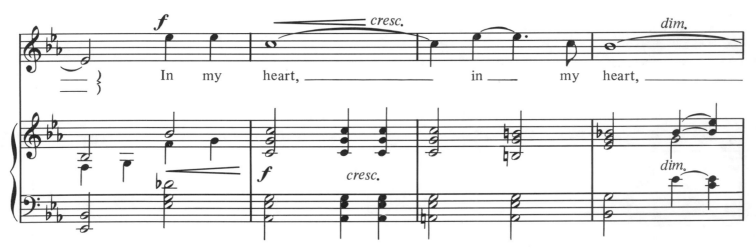

In my heart, ——————— in —— my heart, ———————

F0114

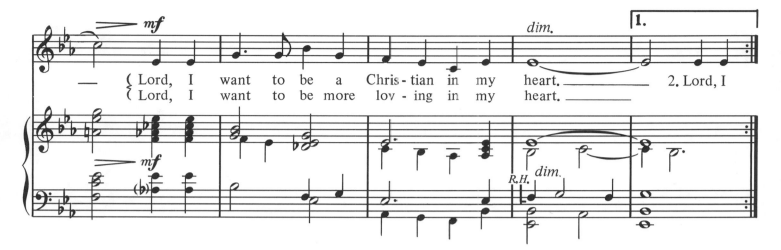

Lord, I want to be a Chris-tian in my heart. ——— 2. Lord, I
Lord, I want to be more lov-ing in my heart. ———

3. Lord, I want to be — like — Je-sus, in my heart, in my

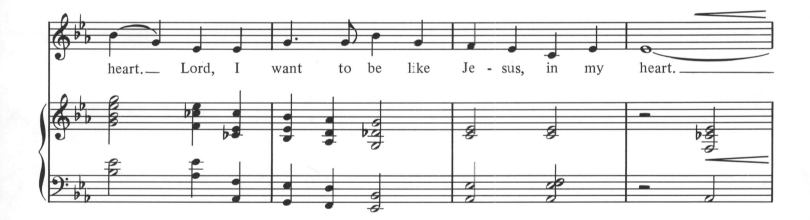

heart. — Lord, I want to be like Je-sus, in my heart. ———

In my heart, ——————— in — my heart, ——————— Lord, I

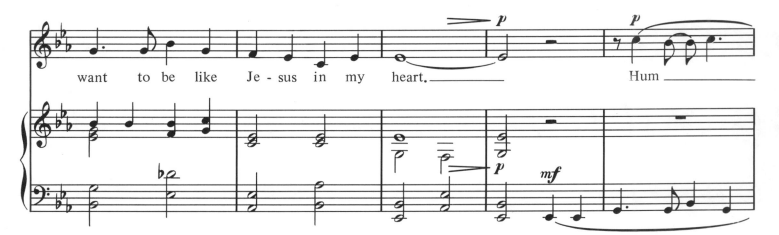

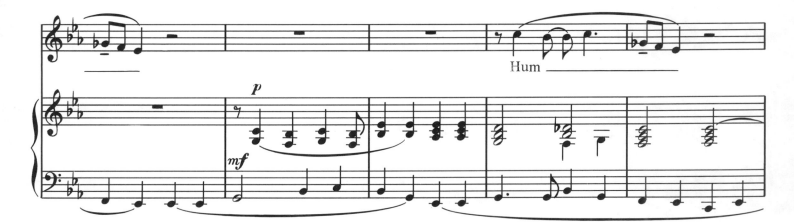

want to be like Je-sus in my heart. Hum

Hum

O, in my heart, in my heart,

Lord, I want to be a Chris-tian in my heart.

* (notes in lower parenthesis for lower voice)

8ba

DONE MADE MY VOW TO THE LORD

TRADITIONAL SPIRITUAL
Arranged by Phillip McIntyre

Done made my vow to the Lord and I nev-er will turn back. I will go, — I shall go to see what the end will be. Done made my vow to the Lord — and I nev-er will

12

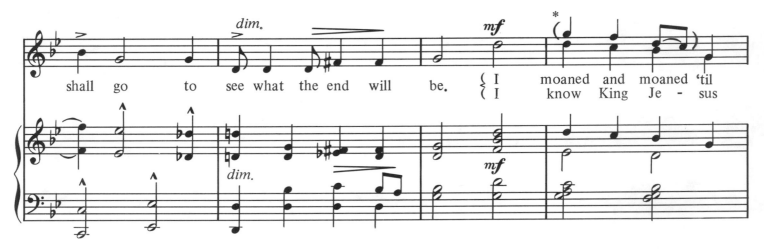

* high notes for verse two

be.   2. When

Lord   and   I   nev - er   will   turn   back. _____   I

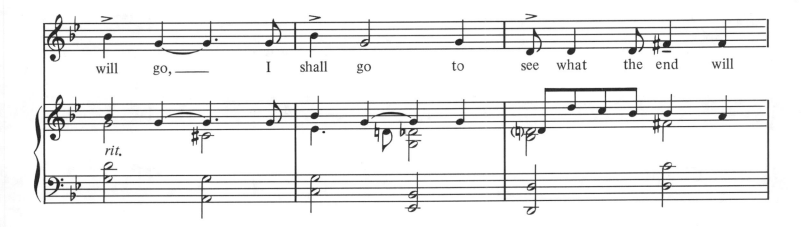

will   go, _____   I   shall   go   to   see   what   the   end   will

be,   see   what   the   end   will   be.

8ba

to William Warfield

Sinner, Please Don't Let This Harvest Pass*

TRADITIONAL SPIRITUAL
Arranged by Phillip McIntyre

Lyrics: Sin - ner, please don't let this har - vest pass. Sin - ner, please don't let this har - vest pass. Sin - ner, please don't let this har - vest pass and die, and lose your soul at last. last.

* Often used at revival meetings.

F0114

Coda

3. I know that my Re - deem - er lives!

I know that my Re - deem - er lives!

I know that my Re - deem - er lives. Sin - ner,

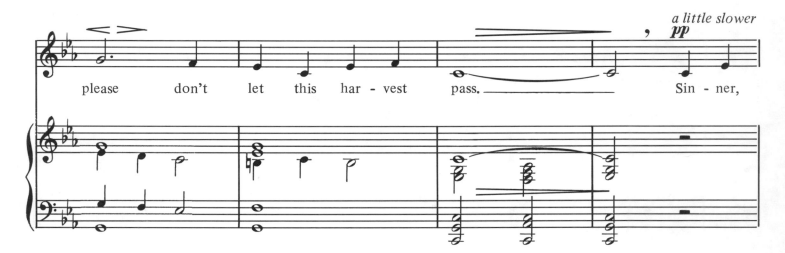

please don't let this har - vest pass. Sin - ner,

to Leontyne Price

YOU BETTER MIND

TRADITIONAL SPIRITUAL
Arranged by Phillip McIntyre

* grace notes to be played on the beat

judge - ment, you bet - ter mind. O, you bet - ter

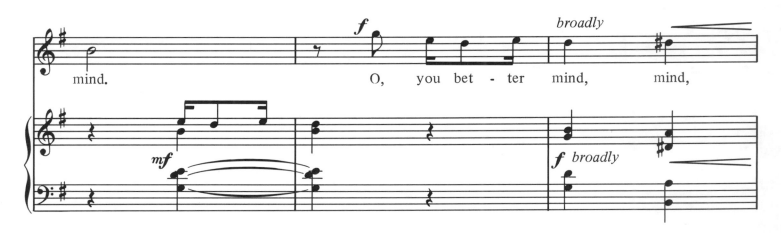

mind. O, you bet - ter mind, mind,

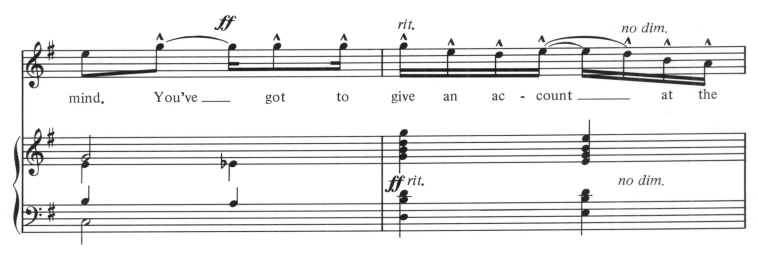

mind. You've ___ got to give an ac - count ___ at the

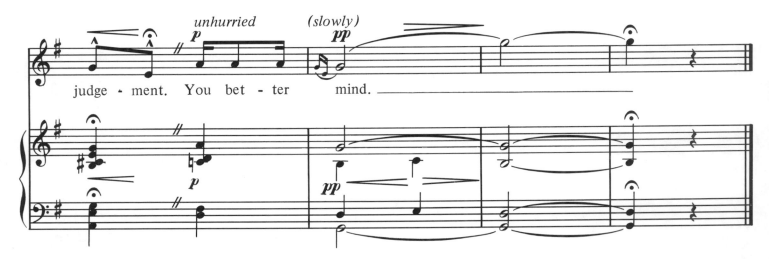

judge - ment. You bet - ter mind. ___

to Valerie Fichelberger

LORD, I DON'T FEEL NO-WAYS TIRED

TRADITIONAL SPIRITUAL
Arranged by Phillip McIntyre

Not Fast, with a steady beat

M.M. ♩ = ca. 60

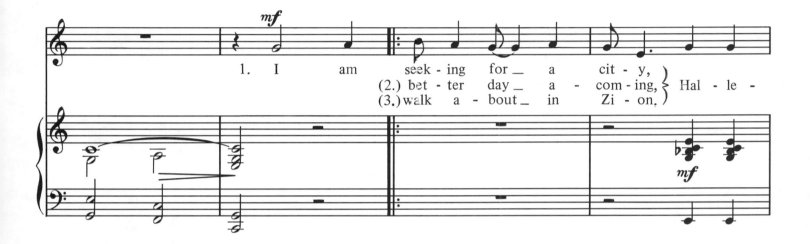

F0114

© Copyright 1990 by H. T. FitzSimons Company. All rights reserved. Made in U.S.A.

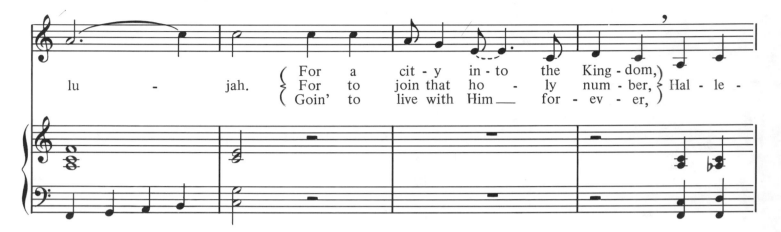

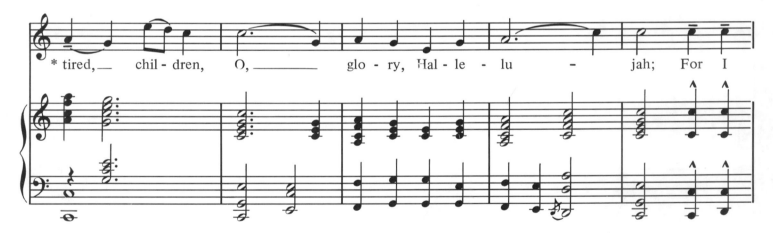

* Pronounced as two syllables - "ti-yad"   ** Pronounced - "fi-ya"

glo - ry, Hal - le - lu - jah. (2. There's a lu - jah. O Lord, I

(3. Goin' to

don't ____ feel _____ no - ways tired, ___ chil - dren, O, _____

glo - ry, Hal - le - lu - jah; For I hope to shout glo - ry when this

world is on fire, ___ chil - dren, O, _____ glo - ry, Hal - le - lu - jah!

to my father, Willie McIntyre

DO LORD, REMEMBER ME!

TRADITIONAL SPIRITUAL
Arranged by Phillip McIntyre

* small notes in parenthesis for vs. 3 & 4.

F0114